Developing Circle Time

by

Teresa Bliss
George Robinson
and
Barbara Maines

copyright **Lucky Duck Publishing Ltd.** 1995

ISBN 1 873942 85 0

Seventh Printing January 2000

CONTENTS

ACKNOWLEDGEMENT.

We would like to thank Jim Ballard for his "Circlebook" (1982). In it we found the first book that went beyond games and activities. It inspired us to begin to look beyond the content of Circle Time and to explore the process and our belief system about the power of the Circle.

Foreword. The meaning of Circles.

Individuals meet to form societies which perform a variety of functions. The purpose of these meetings might be understood by observing the physical formation of the individuals in the group. A naive observer would recognise a view of parliament as an adversarial contest between opposing participants. She would also recognise a court room scene as the imposition of power by high status individuals upon a deviant or rejected member. A discussion held in circular formation or a dance in the round would probably be interpreted as co-operative and non-hierarchical. The image of North American indigents passing the peace pipe around a circle, the link-armed singing of Auld Lang Sine in a circle or even the preparation for war in a circular dance convey a unified purpose shared by all members of the group.

Developing the ideas.

If you are reading this book it is likely that you already have some experience through reading or participation in Circle groups. In the publication Circle Time by Teresa Bliss and Jo Tetley (1993) we described the structure, rules and activities which form the basis of starting and maintaining Circle Time groups. These are only briefly referred to in this publication. It is not until you start to use the processes for yourself that you will discover the fun and the deeper values achieved in Circle Time. In order to convey this more vividly we made a training video called Coming Round to Circle Time (1995). If you have seen this video then you will already be aware of our commitment to and our enthusiasm for Circle Time as an important contribution to the development of altruistic and empathic behaviours, vital to any civilised and peaceful society. In this publication we hope to offer Circle Time enthusiasts some more ideas about extending their work and to answer some of the questions which have arisen in discussion groups.

Circle Time has two main components; content and process. Our first publication dealt mainly with the former and in this one we will put an emphasis on process. As a facilitator you will already have developed your own style and your group will have favourite games and activities. We hope that this publication will help you to increase the value of something that is already rewarding and enjoyable.

Circle Time is now quite likely to be found in British schools as a regular activity for pupils. Writers such as Lawrence (1988), White (1992), Mosley (1993) and Curry & Bromfield (1994) encourage Circle Time as a process that enhances the self-esteem of the participants. Further justification of the use of precious class time can be established by relating the various activities to National Curriculum targets in speaking and listening.

The value of Circle Time lies in the possibility for development and acceptance for the participants rather than in a goal oriented process of problem solving. Because it is easy to begin Circle Time and because it is fun for all those involved, it may be that some users do not consider the values and assumptions that underpin the process. Ballard (1982) identifies ten value statements and suggests that if teachers do not share these they will have difficulty in conducting Circle Time. Whilst not wishing to be as restrictive as Ballard we would ask the reader to consider the beliefs listed below and their intrinsic relationship with the concept of Circle Time.

Our Beliefs.

* Children are essentially good if they are treated with respect.
* Teachers are in a powerful position, responsible for the environment within which children learn.
* This environment should be supportive and accepting if it is to foster the best development of young people.
* Teachers should be thoughtful about their position of power in relation to pupils and should avoid using fear to control behaviour. Fear does not enable and it cannot encourage the development of self-motivated young people.
* Teachers' expectations of the ability and worth of a young person are inevitably transmitted and these expectations will affect the self-image of the young person. The teacher, therefore, has a responsibility to convey acceptance and encouragement.
* If young people are to become self-reliant adults they must be given the opportunity to make choices and the responsibility for the consequences of those choices.
* The ability to make a good decision is dependent on knowledge of self and knowledge of others. In order to achieve this awareness it is important to be able to identify needs of self and needs of the other person and to understand the conflict that may arise in a relationship where these needs are not congruent.
* Understanding of needs and resolution of conflicts depends upon two essential skills: the ability to listen when other people speak and the ability to speak clearly about one's own feelings.

WHAT HAPPENS IN CIRCLE TIME?

The process of Circle Time involves the key skills required by any individual belonging to a social group. Ballard (1982) describes Circle Time as:

1. Awareness - knowing who I am.
2. Mastery - knowing what I can do.
3. Social interaction - knowing how I function in the world of others.

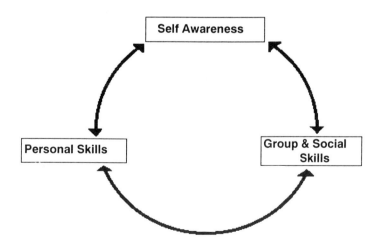

Circle Time is an inter-related, interactive, multi-layered process. Within the Circle participants learn about self, learn about others and relate this knowledge to build relationships between individuals and between groups. The aims for self are to:
* communicate needs
* understand the needs of others
* increase confidence, raise self-esteem.

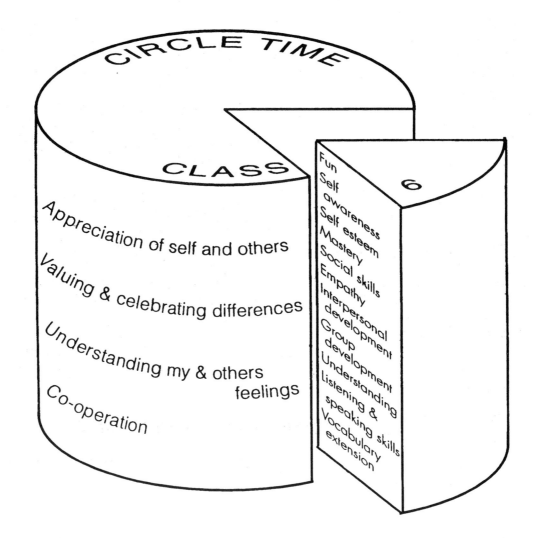

This is a circular, not a linear, process offering a lifelong opportunity for development.

The N.C.C. (1993) publication on spiritual and moral development points out the essential requirements for the development of young people as:

"Self knowledge, relationships, feelings and emotions are an essential part of the spiritual and moral development of young people.

Self knowledge. An awareness of oneself in terms of thoughts, feelings, emotions, responsibilities and experiences; a growing understanding and acceptance of individual identity; the development of self-respect.
Relationships. Recognising and valuing the worth of each individual; developing a sense of community; the ability to build up relationships with others.
Feelings and Emotions. The sense of being moved by beauty or kindness; hurt by injustice or aggression; a growing awareness of when it is important to control emotions and feelings, and how to learn to use such feelings as a source of growth."
(page 3)

These three essential elements from the N.C.C. document can link the skills represented in the first diagram.

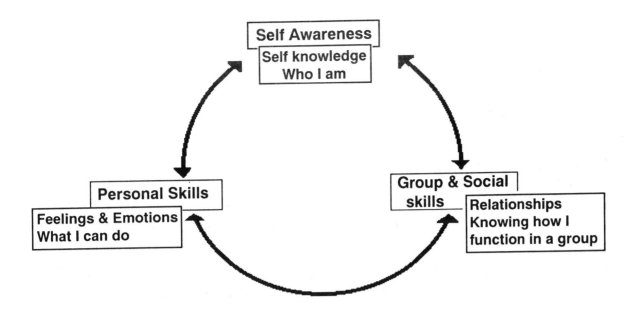

Self awareness : Self knowledge: Who I am.

Circle Time helps young people to become aware of themselves. Until we learn about ourselves we cannot learn about other people. Some of the activities in Circle Time achieve this by encouraging young people to make "I" statements, I like....., I feel..... These are personal statements about self, the rules of Circle Time demand that the group give acceptance to their "I" statements and that they can therefore be made in safety. Whilst one person is making a personal statement the other group members are learning,
* to listen to other people,
* to avoid put-downs and negative statements,
* to respect the need for confidentiality and the boundaries of space and time around the group.

Circle Time provides consent and permission for young people to talk about feelings and emotions, joy and sadness, pain and pleasure. The participants learn about their own feelings and about the feelings of others. They also learn how to express them verbally and non-verbally. The relationships between needs, behaviour and feelings can be explored and these may be focused on particular themes such as friendship, co-operation, loss or conflict. For example,

"When I fall out with a friend I feel......" *"The best day I ever had was ...."*

Ballard (1982) identifies four ways in which Circle Time helps to develop and provides an opportunity to communicate:

* *self understanding*
* *self awareness.*

1. Focusing on a particular topic or statement and understanding its implications.
2. Hearing other people's contributions and comparing them with our own perspectives.
3. Learning to disclose openly only what is comfortable to communicate at that time.
4. To receive feedback by watching and listening to the responses of the group and learning from this feedback.

These processes of open communication and acceptance help the individual participant to reduce the natural and cultural inhibitions we often experience when discussing strong emotions.

Self-Disclosure.

Self-disclosure about feelings, assumptions and beliefs will enable others in the group to have access and therefore insight into the private world of other members. It is a crucial activity within the group and essential for its growth.

The self-disclosure encouraged needs to be kept at a safe level. It is best to start with simple statements such as favourites:

e.g.   TV. programmes
        Foods
        Music.

Even these may be hard for some people. The group's reaction to the disclosure will establish the safety to allow progress to more sensitive information:

e.g.   falling out with a friend
        getting bullied

or even:

        feeling shy
        living in a one parent family.

If a young person discloses the name of a favourite pop group and this is greeted with shrieks of derision then the message is sent that it is not safe to express this view. This will limit the group's opportunity to grow because there will be a taboo on certain subjects or a rejection of certain individuals. The participants fail to function as a unified group because of:

        a lack of trust
        a lack of support and care offered.

Self-disclosure needs to take place at a pace that is appropriate for the group because the reaction of the group will determine the level and extent of genuine disclosures possible in the future. Groups that are mature enough to offer unconditional acceptance will give total support and love to individual members. It is our experience that this can be achieved by young people who are used to the ethos of Circle Time. It is important to remember that self-disclosure is not just about words: - tone of voice and facial expression might indicate that very strong emotions accompany quite neutral words e.g. *I don't like playtime.* There are three important issues that are relevant to self-disclosure.

The Pass Rule.

Children must always be allowed to pass. At the end of the activity go back and give the opportunity to make a comment. If they still choose to pass your message, both verbal and non verbal, must be that passing is always acceptable.

Confidentiality.

You must always stress that the information given within the circle is confidential. You can discuss with the pupils the reason for this.

Being Positive.

Throughout our work we always try to focus on positive aspects of an issue. This is not to say we ignore or hide from negatives. However, we are clear that some negatives are unacceptable. We would never knowingly ask children to make disclosures about which they may be embarrassed or teased or regret later. Circle Time can deal with issues such as bullying, friendship patterns and theft. We have seen this done sensitively and badly. Never ask children to name names or to admit to misdemeanours. Concentrate on feelings.

> *"If somebody stole from me I'd feel...."*
> *"A victim of bullying might feel...."*

If negatives arise try to turn them into positives, in areas such as bullying move towards what pupils might do in the future,

> *"The next time I see bullying happening I will ...."*

Silent Statements/ Partners.

Some children find it very difficult to talk in the circle. They feel exposed and threatened. Using Silent Statements enables them to make declarations about themselves without the need for words.

Many of the games encourage children to speak well of themselves. They are asked to say what they enjoy and what they are good at. Adults as well as children become uncomfortable when they think they will be seen to be boasting. Sharing information with a partner is one way of overcoming this reluctance to celebrate achievements and skills. It is much less threatening to disclose success to one person than to a group of thirty. The other will find it easier to identify to the group what her partner is good at. This type of activity is very useful in the early stages of Circle Time to assist self-disclosure.

Another reason is to encourage the pupils to know one another better. In most classes pupils will know one or two friends very well and know very little about the other classmates. By using silent statements or a mixing up game friends who will want to sit together can be separated and partners will discover information about others who they don't know so well.

Group pressure to conform.

At first pupils may co-operate with the games simply because it is the activity the group has been directed to do. They may feel awkward, shy, silly or uncomfortable. Their feelings will be expressed in body language and tone of voice, while their words will be fulfilling the obligation to the task in hand. As group members become familiar with the task of speaking publicly about information which is not usually disclosed, their discomfort with unfamiliar activities will disappear. They will begin to trust themselves and others and as the individuals relax so will the group.

Whilst there may be an age factor related to the development of Circle Time skills, we believe that a much more significant factor is the opportunity to experience the Circle Time process and to become comfortable with self disclosing and listening. A group of nine year olds who have been used to Circle Time might display less inhibition and more self awareness than a group of twelve year olds beginning Circle Time as a new experience.

GROUP AND SOCIAL SKILLS : RELATIONSHIPS : KNOWING HOW I FUNCTION IN A GROUP.

As participants become more confident as speakers and listeners they will have opportunities to observe and understand that communication is powerful and underpins process and social function. In pair and group activities young people can experience the effects of what is said on others. This can be learned from experience as an observer, a receiver or a sender of communication within the group.

One group asked a particular boy to leave the room and in his absence they made a list of positive statements about him. He was not popular and some young people had to think hard to find something nice to say. They all managed it. When he returned the list was read out to him. He was pleased and said that he particularly liked the comment made by a girl, "He is good at football." That evening the girl told her mother that she felt much more positively about this boy because he chose her comment as his favourite. The activity had produced reciprocal good feelings as receiving and sending roles were exchanged.

Quite young children can begin to understand their responsibility for the effects of what they say and its significance for friendships, co-operation and conflict resolution. During the life of a circle group this process explored through completion statements might progress from safe examples such as; "A friend is......" "I feel upset when......" to statements which explore personal and group dynamics such as; "Somebody felt sorry for me when......" "The time I did something that others didn't like was......" "The time I made somebody angry was........"

GROUP DEVELOPMENT.

When using this method of working there will be a process the group has to go through to move from being a collection of individuals, which sadly many classes remain, to a cohesive group able to work in a truly co-operative collaboration. The games suggested in this book and others, such as Bliss and Tetley (1993), Fountain (1990), Canfield and Wells (1976) and Curry & Bromfield (1994) will give the class teacher a framework that facilitates the group process outlined below.

It is our experience that few classes have the opportunity to become truly cohesive learning groups. It is not an uncommon experience for children not to know the names of some of their classmates when we introduce the name game. Even where they do know all the names of the children in their class, they know very little about their peers, other than those they regularly sit with or socialise with. While the process of discovery about one another is both illuminating and enjoyable, its value to the teacher goes deeper.

The concept for the circle is that everyone is equal with the same right to be listened to, accepted and respected. The teacher at first leads the group. She will set the level of expectations for the social norms and values. However, as the group develops and evolves into a state of maturity, the teacher will find that the students have internalised the group norms, pupils and teacher taking equal ownership and responsibility for the care and support of individual members. When a Circle Time group has reached this stage of development the children will be able to function with a high degree of autonomy and self determination in a way that is acceptable to the school. Before a group's evolution arrives at this point there are recognisable developmental stages that all groups go through.

Johnson & Johnson (1987:361) discuss the work of Tuckman (1965) whose review of the studies of group development revealed a surprising amount of agreement on the stages that group growth goes through. He noted four basic stages labelled:

Stage 1 - Forming
Stage 2 - Storming
Stage 3 - Norming
Stage 4 - Performing.

Stage 1. Forming.

This is a formative stage whereby the processes, rules and procedures will be learnt and understood. Individual members will establish their place. The overt rules of Circle Time are explained in Bliss and Tetley (1993). Behind the overt rules are the beliefs and assumptions that translate into a list of covert rules such as:

* *we are all individually responsible for ourselves*
* *the group is collectively responsible for each member*
* *the group should be supportive, facilitating and caring at all times*
* *the group is a safe place to be.*

It is during this time that the issue of confidentiality may be discussed if appropriate. The rules of Circle Time will evolve appropriately as children grow and develop. Older students may wish to discuss topics that they agree to confine to Circle Time or to keep confidential within the class or tutor group.

In this early stage of group growth the teacher will make decisions about the appropriateness of rules and determine what they should be. Later the group will be sufficiently competent to take those decisions. Even at this early stage children should be asked their opinions about the rules and have the opportunity to feel a part of the teacher's decision making process. The explanation of the thoughts and the reasons given will help formulate the children's own thought process. Hence the need for a positive role model at all times. The rule for "no put downs" applies also to the teacher. For example it would be wholly inappropriate for a teacher to say something like, *"Because some of you have made such silly suggestions, I will decide..."* There will always be sensible or positive suggestions from some. Focus on those. Therefore a more appropriate phrasing would be, *"Thank you for your suggestions about how we should go from here and from what some of you have said I believe we could..."*

Creating a feeling of safety within the group will encourage trust. Modelling acceptance will be copied. As individuals feel valued then they will be able to value one another. This will lay foundations for later, when the group begins to make decisions and attempts to resolve difficult or sensitive issues.

Stage 2. Storming.

The road to self autonomy is bumpy, fraught with difficulties and conflicts. Such is the nature of this stage. It is the beginning of the transition from dependence on external authority to reliance on self determination and internal control. This is the equivalent, in terms of group development, of the teenage years. Individuals wishing to retain their own identity will often choose to do it by challenging the authority of the teacher and through conflict with one another. It is an essential stage in the life of the group. It is a difficult stage for a teacher but an excellent chance to fully demonstrate the ethos of Circle Time through acceptance. It is important that the teacher uses mediation, negotiation and problem solving by the group, rather than revert to overt extrinsic controls that deny the students the opportunity to gain ownership of the resolution of problems and thus develop a greater internalised commitment to the group.

Stage 3. Norming.

This is the completion of the transition phase. The modelling of acceptance, the work on development of trust, self worth and commitment will pay off at this stage. The group will have reached a level of maturity whereby the group norms will be internalised by individuals. Regulation within the group will be internally driven rather than externally imposed. Individuals will not only have more internalised commitment to the group but also to one another. The will and ability to care for and support one another will be enhanced because they will know, through the development of trust, that their efforts will be accepted rather than rejected.

Stage 4. Performing.

Groups who have reached this level will be capable of functioning with a high degree of autonomy. There will be mutual respect between members enabling them to address conflicts of interest, controversial and problematic issues, while taking care not to cause undue or damaging distress to the relationships within the group. In a group performing with such a degree of maturation all members will feel empowered to ask for help and take turns. It will be automatic to facilitate and maximise the learning of others within the group. It will be possible to share leadership in some circumstances with the teacher moving to the role of consultant.

Attainment of stage 4 will not be easy or automatic. It will depend on many complex factors. The teacher requires the skill to lead the group successfully through stage 2 to "co-operative interdependence". Group members require, or need the opportunity to learn, the necessary interactive skills for effective group participation.

Beyond Stage 4.

Many adult groups that form have a natural life with an ebb and flow. This is also the case for class groups. If something changes within the group - for example someone leaves, a new child comes or there is a change of teacher, then the group may well need to go through a period, considerably shorter than the first time of reforming, storming and norming until it has reached once again an ability to maximise all members' performances.

Other Developmental Factors.

Tuckman's work was mainly based on research into adult groups. Circle Time is aimed at young people from the age of five to eighteen. The speed at which the group is able to proceed through the stages, and the level it will achieve, is dependent on many factors such as the ages of the group members, their ability to understand and carry out verbal instructions, their level of articulation, their previous experience of this type of work, the culture of the school they are in and so on.

Many of the exercises teachers do with their classes will take them in to unfamiliar territory, not only for themselves as people but in comparison with the type of work children and their teachers are used to experiencing together in the classroom situation. It will be possible for a teacher in a primary school to reach a level of co-operation, support and empathy that will surprise many people. Experience has shown that when a class group achieves an ability to work with a sensitive, caring and supportive attitude to one another, it continues to deepen as they mature.

Each age will bring with it different problems. The dynamics of the group may need to be adjusted, some reforming may take place. Some conflict will arise during that time but a class group used to listening, taking account of individual needs and attempting to meet those needs within the context of the group will manage the period of conflict with greater tolerance and maturity than a group with no such experience. It has to be said that some conflict is necessary for growth. If it is well handled with compassion through mediation and/or negotiation then the group will survive to be stronger and more united. Conflict that is poorly handled in a punitive and judgmental way will result in angry children, frustrated teachers and continuing conflicts that will bubble up in expected and unexpected ways. A mature Circle Time group will be one that has reached the ability to self regulate with the teacher operating for some of the time as an equal member and for the rest of the time as consultant. The need for her to impose external control and discipline will have been left behind.

Personal skills : Feelings and emotions : What can I do?

When one person attempts to convey an idea, an explanation or meaning to another she has in her mind a myriad of facts, feelings and detail. This information is translated and delivered to the other in the form of words, body language, facial expression, tone of voice and gesture. The receiver understands it only in the context of her knowledge of the sender, her experiences and her personal experience of language. The chance that this process achieves 100% accurate shared understanding of meaning is infinitely small.

When the content of the message is factual there is a greater chance that it can be accurately conveyed..." *I have brought your book back.*" When feelings are communicated both the expression and understanding are more difficult and more susceptible to misunderstandings..." *I hate parties.*"

Whilst it is important to convey both facts and feelings we often find in a particularly British use of language, a confusion between these two aspects of language. For example you might hear one person say to another, *"I felt you didn't support me at the meeting last night.*"In this sentence the speaker is not expressing a feeling but a cognitive thought. The sentence might more accurately be expressed as, *"I think or know that you did not support me at the meeting last night and I felt upset or irritated."*

In Circle Time young people become used to expressing genuine feelings and extend the vocabulary they commonly use for this purpose. The process of expressing and understanding the meaning of any communication is the most vital skill that any of us require as we become effective communicators. Circle Time provides the ideal opportunity to learn these skills, to practise them in a safe environment and to model the skills we have to other learners.

Non verbal communication.

Non verbal communication as with verbal communication is a skill that can be developed. One of the features of the Circle is the way the group members listen. As one person is speaking the rest of the Circle will be not only listening but usually everybody is looking at the speaker. Pupils will improve their skills in observing body language, facial expressions and voice intonation.

Some of the early activities such as Passing the Squeeze or Passing the Smile can assist the pupils to learn to look into somebody's face or hold somebody's hand without embarrassment.

Self-esteem.

Self-esteem has been a focus in much of our work. We believe that pupils who have a positive view of themselves are more likely to achieve more, both socially and academically, than those pupils whose self-esteem is low. Self-esteem seems to be a pre-requisite for a self-disciplined and self-motivated person. The process of Circle Time allows the young person to learn more about herself and move away from an egocentric position. From this self knowledge comes the ability to recognise the needs of others.

We accept that there are several significant others in the pupils' lives, and some of the class members may come from less than encouraging and supportive home backgrounds. The teacher must accept that she still has an important role to play. Aspects of self-esteem are situationally specific and the total environment of the school, and not just Circle Time, should be planned to demonstrate to all pupils that they are unique, acceptable, cared for and valued.

Summary.

Circle Time is a very powerful and enjoyable process that assists both the development of the individual and the individual as a member of the group. The diagram indicates in a circular way the various elements of the inter-related processes.

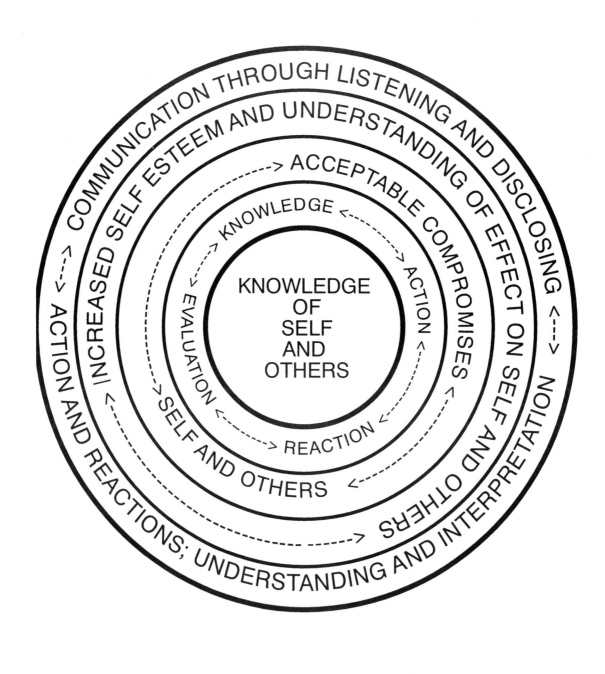

1. Circle Time should generate a sense of belonging which promotes acceptance and support within the community of the class and school.

2. Circle Time facilitates the growth of self-esteem through public acknowledgement and acceptance of individuals as well as through public celebrations of abilities and achievements.

3. Circle Time encourages the use of a variety of inter-personal skills, listening to others and accepting different viewpoints. This demands the development of cognitive and social competence resulting in both individual and group maturation.

4. Circle Time is enjoyed even by the most difficult pupils. It generates positive peer pressure for behaviour which helps the group to function more effectively.

5. Circle Time allows the forum to explore negative and destructive feelings with the opportunity for peers to provide positive help and support to one another.

6. Circle Time facilitates understanding of individual group members through insights gained during the process. This broadens their perspectives and opens up their knowledge of alternative views on life by making them aware of the variety of experiences, strategies and beliefs people bring to everyday life.

Circle Time may eventually offer a group a framework for addressing problems. However, it should not be confused with Quality Circles. These originated in Japanese industry and are a specific technique for problem solving.

FACILITATOR'S SKILLS.

Listening and Acceptance.

Pupils may sometimes make comments that the teacher feels she should respond to,

"I like to hurt my sister."

She can accept the statement and move onto the next pupil or she may say, *"I haven't given you much time to think. I'll come back to you later."*

Circle Time is about listening and accepting. It is not appropriate to make comments such as,

"I can't agree with that."

"That's silly."

It is not an Advice Group or Sympathy Group or Therapy Group.

Advice, sympathy and solutions have no place within the Circle, the following would not be acceptable,

"I know what you are saying, I felt the same when....."

"That's terrible, I think you were very brave."

"Why don't you try....."

"If that had happened to me I'd have done....."

We should never seek further details,

"And what happened then?"

"Who did that to make you feel....?"

We may be presented with information that is painful and we feel that we have to respond. Children might make comments like:

"I get sad when I don't see my dad."

"I get sad when my mum shouts at my dad."

It is best to accept and to move on. Circle Time is a group process and an understanding and acceptance of the feelings may be sufficient. The process is intended to help an individual to be aware of her feeling and to learn ways to express feelings in a safe environment.

One Deputy Head in a primary school decided he was going to deal with bullying. He used silent statements then went on to sentence completion, *"Something that makes me sad is.."* Six of the twenty eight children said they were sad when they didn't see their dad or mum when they were supposed to. He thought he had prepared them to disclose about bullying. However their sadness at the absence of a parent was uppermost in their minds. He was taken aback by what he heard but dealt with it by acknowledging the sadness expressed by so many. He felt it was inappropriate to continue with bullying so he finished the session early with an ending activity. At a later stage he gave the class the opportunity to write and draw something important to them. Only one child chose to write about absent parents. We believe giving pupils the opportunity to acknowledge a problem and hearing that their problem is a shared problem satisfied a need and helped reduce the problem.

Picking things up later.

If a comment is made that you feel you must do something about you will need to do this privately. You could use active listening skills that are based on feelings rather than facts. Do not interrogate and provide the opportunity for the pupil to refuse to disclose if she wishes to remain silent. An opening comment might be,

> *"You said in Circle Time you were sad when ..., would you like to tell me more?"*
> *"When you said ....., I thought you were feeling,.... Would you like to talk about it?"*

If you realise the child is making disclosures about abuse then you must not ask questions at this time. You must follow your school/authority procedures.

We must remember that the pupil did not choose to be part of the group and cannot choose to leave. Within this context we have to accept the comments the individual chooses to make. We have to create safety from ridicule, embarrassment and teasing. You will do this within the circle and we find that this spreads into other aspects of school life.

Circle Time seems to work on several levels at once. The crucial aim is to help each individual to develop into a member of a group of people committed to one another, able to accept and value individual differences. Essential to this is the ability to feel good about oneself as an individual and as a member of the group.

If you are interested in Active Listening we recommend Gordon T, (1974) Teacher Effectiveness Training.

GETTING STARTED.

Rules.

We believe the rules for Circle Time should be kept to a minimum, e.g., no more than one or two at a session. We usually only introduce the first rule. Sometimes the first and second rules are all that is required for a group to run well. However, we suggest you allow the rules to evolve as necessary. The same rule sometimes needs to be introduced time and again in different contexts and for particular individuals, but this is after all how we teach anything. Below is a list of rules we used from time to time, but we want to emphasise they may not all be needed.

We listen when someone else is speaking.

We may pass.

We don't remind anyone else what they should be doing.

There are no "put downs."

The pass rule is best introduced as discretely as possible. You will find some children like to test the pass rule for one or two rounds. The novelty soon wears off.

Organisation of Circle Time.

It is best done in the classroom where you can keep the warm atmosphere you generate. The beginning or end of a period is the easiest time to rearrange chairs and desks. We would recommend that chairs are placed in a circle, leaving the centre free for movement within the circle. If the children are seated on the floor, as they get up and move around, the circle becomes distorted and the space they need to return to is lost. Opportunities for listening and eye-contact between all participants is a priority. We have found that the session runs much more smoothly when children are comfortable.

The activities should last for about twenty minutes to half an hour. Each session should begin with an opening and end with a closing - a familiar and safe game or activity which encloses the session. Even when time is running short it is important not to close in a rush without a symbolic "Good-bye."

Introduce new activities.

You may be familiar with Circle Time (Bliss and Tetley 1993) or have worked from some of the other publications which introduce the basic games and activities. The next section builds on the ideas in the starter books. You might also find the video, "Coming Round to Circle Time" useful .

DEVELOPING CIRCLE TIME.

At first teachers who are new to the process experiment and play with it in an unstructured way. Their experience of a warm, relaxed supportive atmosphere where the pupils seem to have fun in a non-competitive way provides the motivation to explore Circle Time further. Once you feel your pupils are beginning to be more caring and supportive you will be able to explore themes. The games element takes a smaller part and discussion becomes more important and more significant. When this starts to

17

happen you need to ensure that everybody gets the opportunity to comment. Always ensure that each session has at least one sentence completion exercise. The aim of this next section is to help you and your pupils develop the skills to be able to move onto issues, conflict resolution and to be able to negotiate the content of the sessions. They will develop self-confidence and a belief in their ability to express feelings in an atmosphere where they will be accepted and listened to.

PLANNING AND RECORDING.

Once you have decided to make Circle Time part of your approach to teaching and learning you need to make it a planned and structured activity.

We have provided an example of a term's work which we hope will give you a model for planning and recording. All groups are unique so make adjustments as necessary.

Term 1.

Aims:

* *To bond the class group.*
* *To build the self-esteem of every group member.*
* *To increase confidence to speak about personal concerns in the group.*
* *To increase the ability to listen to others.*

As the class becomes more confident about speaking in the group and learning to listen to others you can add other skills such as,

* *Ability to respond empathically to others*
* *Ability to understand non verbal behaviour*
* *Awareness of bullying.*

The plan for the term gives one way of planning and recording. We have listed some of the aspects that are covered in the activities. This will help you provide a balanced range of activities.

Key.

1   Say name aloud/introduce self to group
2   Affirmation of self
3   Positive affirmation
4   Mixing the group
5   Giving information about self to group
6   Self awareness/social interaction
7   Making eye contact
8   Group affirmation
9   Fun
10 Co-operation
11 Affirmation to a friend
12 Positive information, one to another
13 Sequencing
14 Taking the lead in a group
15 Taking a public risk of failure
16 Listening
17 Trust
18 Body language.

You can add new aspects as and when necessary.

Session	Game	Purpose	Game	Purpose	Game	Purpose	Game	Purpose	Game	Purpose
1	Name game	1, 2, 16	Silent statements	2, 4, 5	Sentence completion	2, 5, 6, 16, 17	Pass the smile	7, 9, 10, 18		
2	Name game	1, 2, 16	Silent statements	2, 4, 5	Sentence completion	2, 5, 6, 16, 17	Information sharing	2, 3, 5, 6,7,10, 11,12,16,17	Pass the squeeze	9, 10, 13, 18
3	Name game	1, 2, 16	Salad bowl	4, 9, 10, 16	Information sharing	2, 3, 5, 6, 10, 11, 12, 16	Follow the leader	6, 7, 13, 14,15		
4	Name game	1, 2, 16	Information sharing	3, 5, 6, 10, 16, 17	Sentence completion	5, 6	Guarding the keys	9, 15, 16	Thunder	9, 10, 13,16
5	Name association	1, 2, 5, 6, 16, 17	Postman	4, 9, 10, 16	Mirrors	6, 10, 13, 14, 17	50 ways of moving	6, 9, 16	Thunder	9, 10, 13,16
6	Name association	1, 2, 5, 6, 16, 17	Silent statements	5, 6,	Sentence completion	2, 3, 5, 6,	Let's laugh	7, 8, 9, 10		
7	Name association	1, 2, 5, 6, 16, 17	Finger Talk	9, 10, 13	Partners	3, 5, 6, 7, 10, 11, 12, 16	Sentence completion	6,9	Pass the squeeze	9, 10, 13
8	Mixing up game	4, 9, 10, 16	Silent statements	2, 3, 5, 6	Finger Talk	9, 10,13, 15	Sentence completion	2, 5, 6	Chinese whispers	9, 10, 13, 16
9	Postman	4, 9, 10, 13, 16	Mirror game	2, 6, 7, 10, 13,17,18	Let's laugh	7, 9, 10,	Sentence completion	2, 5, 6	Thunder	9, 10, 13,16
10	Salad bowl	4, 9, 10, 16	Web of friendship	8, 11, 12, 16	Sentence completion	5, 6, 17				

Session 1.

Name Game.

Keep this very simple the first time and ask the children to introduce themselves and say their own name out loud.

Silent Statements.

Say *"Change places those who................"* then choose something appropriate for your age group, for example:

Infants... are wearing black shoes, can ride a bike, have lost a tooth.

Juniors.... are wearing trainers, watch Neighbours, enjoy swimming, went away on holiday.

Secondary...... are wearing sweatshirts, are wearing earrings, watch The Bill, walk to school.

Adults.....are wearing a watch, have been to the theatre recently, enjoy a glass of wine.

Sentence Completion.

Choose from the hundreds of sentence completions listed later in this book.

Pass the Smile.

The children try to keep "blank" faces. The facilitator starts by passing a smiling "mask" to a child beside her who smiles and passes on her mask. A fun way to end Circle Time.

Areas covered in this section 1, 2, 4, 5, 6, 7, 9, 10, 16, 17, 18.

Session 2.

Name Game.

Introduce self and person to left or right.

Silent Statements.

Choose something that is appropriate for your age group as suggested for the last session.

Sentence Completion.

This is the time you will focus on your theme for the session. Choose a theme and have one, two or three sentence completions prepared. It is advisable not to have too many in a row because the children become fidgety waiting for their next turn.

Information Sharing (pairs).

Some children and adults find it threatening to state to the whole class that they are good at something. It is not something we, in our culture, are encouraged to do. By sharing information with just one person who then shares the information with the rest of the group we can benefit from the affirmation without the fear of inhibition.

Pass the Squeeze.

The group holds hands. The facilitator squeezes the hand of the person to the left or right and the squeeze goes round. This is a co-operative exercise that is affirming.

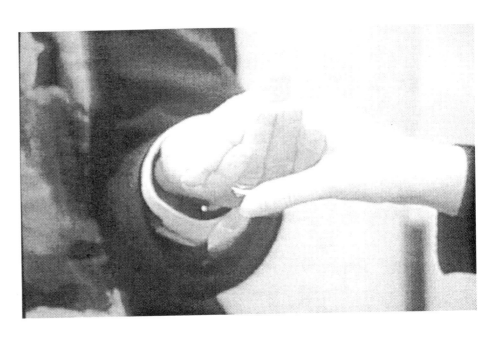

Areas covered in this session   1, 2, 3, 4, 5, 6, 7, 9, 10, 11, 12, 13, 16, 17.

SESSION 3.

Name Game.

Introduce person to the right, yourself and person to the left.

Salad Bowl (or another Mixing up Game).

Divide children by vegetable names - always three e.g. lettuce, tomato, cucumber. This gives you quite a lot of control over who sits where. When you call the name of the vegetable all those with the names, e.g. tomato, change places. When you call "Salad Bowl" everyone changes places. The purpose of this game is to really mix the children, to encourage them to sit with children they do not normally sit with. One of the aims of Circle Time is to encourage class members to know more about children they do not normally mix with. At the end of this game you should have a well mixed Salad Bowl and can proceed to a pair activity.

Information Sharing.

Put the members of the group into pairs and ask them to find out two things they both like and then to report back to the group, each person saying *"We both like..."*

Follow the Leader.

This is primarily a fun game. One child is chosen as the "leader" while another is out of the room. The child returns to the centre of the circle. The leader makes small foot, hand, eye, head movements. Everyone copies, while the child in the middle tries to guess the leader.

Areas covered in this session   1, 2, 3, 4, 5, 6, 7, 8, 9, 10, 11 12, 13, 14, 15, 16.

SESSION 4.

This week's session is devoted exclusively to listening.

Name Game.

We suggest that the group members might be ready to introduce themselves and say how they are feeling. Some children feel silly and awkward doing this for the first time.

Information Sharing.

This is a simple listening exercise. It is helpful to say to the listener "pretend you have sticking plaster over your mouth". It can also be used to think about non-verbal clues such as use of eyes and body language. One child listens to another without interruption. Then they change roles.

Sentence Completion.

Two sentences about listening such as :-

> *"A good listener is someone who....."*

"A person who is a good listener is....."

Guarding the Keys.

Everyone in the group keeps their eyes closed whilst one child has to collect a bunch of keys from somewhere in the circle without being heard.

Thunder.

The teacher tells a story about a rainstorm making clapping rhythms that grow louder, then softer. The children copy.

Areas covered in this session   1, 2, 3, 5, 6, 9, 10, 13, 15, 16, 17.

SESSION 5.

This session includes work on body language/body awareness.

Name Association.

Each child talks about name. *"I like/I don't like my name because......"*

Postman.

This game has the most potential for the teacher to control the seating arrangements in the group. All the children are numbered. The teacher can call out odd or even numbers, a string of numbers or just two. Everyone changes when collection time is called.

Mirrors.

This game does sometimes bring out feelings of irritation and hostility so it is important that the teacher plans the seating arrangements with this in mind by using a mixing up game such as Postman. The game encourages observation and copying of body language and is described later in the text.

50 ways of moving.

This is another fun way of raising awareness of their bodies and how they move. Children have to move across the circle in as many different and imaginative ways as possible.

Areas covered in this session 1, 2, 3, 4, 5, 6, 9, 10, 13, 14, 16, 17.

SESSION 6.

This should be a consolidation week.

Name Association.

Extend the work you did in session 5 with a sentence completion.. *"I would like my name to have been....."*

Silent Statements.

Have two relevant reasons for changing places. Suggestions are listed later in the text.

Sentence Completion.

Use two or three sentences designed to help self-confidence.

Let's Laugh.

The purpose of this activity is enjoyment. Children from nursery to secondary ages have to try to make each other giggle. It's fun. Playing and having fun together are important ways to bond members of a group.

Areas covered in this section. 1, 2, 3, 5, 6, 7, 8, 9, 10, 16, 17.

SESSION 7.

Name Association.

This extends the activity about names already developed in sessions 5 and 6. Extend the sentence completion with *"I wish my name had been.....because....."*

[Note: You may wish to play a Mixing up Game before you play the next game.]

Finger Talk.

This provides another method of non-verbal communication. We normally rely on hearing and speaking. This game uses neither. The facilitator draws a picture with her finger on the back of one child who in turn draws the same picture on the next child and so on around the circle until the message has travelled the whole way round. Keep the picture simple or the activity will take too long to pass round the circle.

Partners.

Using the sentence completion choose one or two relevant topics for children to share with each other.

Sentence Completion.

Choose a fun sentence completion such as *"If I were an animal....."* or *"If I had one wish....."*

Pass the squeeze.

Areas covered in this session. 1, 2, 3, 5, 6, 7, 8, 9, 10, 11, 12, 13, 16, 17.

SESSION 8.

This session will explore alternatives to communication through a channel other than speaking or listening. It will also explore perceptions. Finger talk game three and Chinese Whispers are the same type of communication game using different channels. See later pages for more details on finger talk.

Areas covered in this session 2, 3, 4, 5, 6, 9, 10, 13, 15, 16.

SESSION 9.

We suggest that you start with Postman in order to mix the children up in an acceptable way. Mirrors Game is a very intense game. After this game do something light and fun, we have suggested Thunder.

Areas covered in this session. 2, 4, 5, 6, 7, 9, 10, 13, 16, 18.

SESSION 10.

The central focus of this final game is the Web of Friendship. It takes a long time, at least twenty minutes possibly thirty. We suggest you encourage friends to sit across the room from one another. If time allows finish with a sentence completion *"While I was waiting for my turn I felt....."*

Areas covered in this session. 4, 5, 6, 8, 9, 10, 11, 12, 13, 16, 17.

Sentence Completion Themes.

Sentence completion is a core activity. Choose two or three sentences that work on the same theme. Choose sentences that are appropriate for your age group or use them as a basis to develop your own sentences.

In the early stages your group will be learning the skills to:
* Speak publicly and develop confidence in themselves.
* Develop their vocabulary to express their thoughts and feelings.

In the early stages the children tend to copy each other. Over time you will see the progress they make in becoming confident to speak for themselves.

Group and Social Skills.
Friendship.
1. A friend is.....
2. A quality I look for in a friend is......
3. Something I like to do with a group of friends is......
4. Something I like to do with my best friend is......
5. The sort of people I like best are....
6. The sort of person I would trust is....
7. I respect friends who.....
8. If a friend has deceived me.....
9. The way I show my friends I'm angry is......
10. I laugh with my friends about......
11. Something my friends do that makes me laugh is.....
12. The kind of behaviour I would expect from my friends towards me is......
13. The kind of behaviour I prefer to see from my friends when we are out is.....
14. If my friends fall out I try to get them back together by....
15. An irritating habit that would turn me off could be....
16. Friends take advantage when.....
17. I take advantage of friends when.....
18. I feel let down by friends when......
19. I have been pleasantly surprised by friends who....
20. If I got married I would want my partner to be......
21. The sort of friend I believe I am is......
22. I would be a better friend if I.....
23. With my friends I see myself mainly a leader/follower.
24. I would not help my friends if.....
25. The most difficult thing about making a new friend is.....
26. The most difficult thing about starting a friendship with someone of the opposite sex is....
27. With my friends I see myself mainly as a giver/receiver.
28a. If I disagree with my friends I.......
28b. I find it easy/difficult to disagree with my friends
29. One thing I believe my friends would say about me is....
30. I get friends to do what I want by....
31. In the past a time I felt left out was........
32. In the past I have left someone out by......

Community.
1. The person I most admire in school is.....
2. The person I most admire in my community is.....
3a. The sort of person I am inspired by is....
3b. The sort of person I am inspired by is..... because.......
4a. At home the sort of person I am is......
4b. With my friends the sort of person I am is....
4c. With teachers the sort of person I am is.....
5. I wish teachers would.....

6. The sort of teachers I admire are.....
7. One thing I would like to change about this school is......
8. One thing I would like to change about this class is.....
9. The best thing about where I live is....
10. The worst thing about where I live is.....

Family.
1. The way I show my family I'm angry is.....
2. Something I admire about my Mum/Dad/parents is.....
3. A good time I had with my family was.....
4. I could laugh with my Mum/Dad about......
5. I could laugh with my brothers/sisters about....
6. The thing I admire about my (sibling) is......
7. The thing that annoys me most about my (sibling) is......
8. I'm most proud of.....
9a. I'm good/not good at being on my own when......
9b. When I'm on my own I prefer to....
10a. I feel my parents/siblings take advantage of me when.....
10b. I take advantage of my parents/siblings when.....
11a. The family member I would most like to be is......
11b. The family member I would most like to be is.....because....
12. I wish my parents would......
13. When I argue with my parents they....
14. When I argue with my parents I.....
15. When I argue with my (sibling) I.....
16. When I argue with my (sibling) my parents.......
17. Something I rely on my family for is.......
18. Something I would miss about my (sibling) is.....
19. Something I would miss about my Mum/Dad is......
20. I still need adults for..........

Self Awareness - Self Knowledge - This is me.
1. One way I am different from other pupils is....
2. One way I am the same as other pupils is.....
3. I sometimes wonder how.......
4. I sometimes wonder why.....
5. I sometimes wonder if.......
6. I believe in....
7. ....is important to me.
8. Someone I hope to be like is....
9. Someone I hope to be like is..........because.....
10. I am worried by....
11. When I leave this school I hope people will remember me as......
12. The sort of person I see myself as is....
13. The kind of person I am influenced by is.....
14. The kind of person I look up to is......
15. I am not pleased with myself when......
16. A time I was brave was......
17. A fear I have overcome was.....
18. A fear I would like to overcome is.........
19 I worry about...
20. If I were Prime Minister I would......
21. If I could make changes in this world I would......
22. What I think about death is.......
23. Religion means.............to me.
24. Something that makes me sad/happy/miserable/angry is.....

25. Something I intend achieving is.......
26. Something I have achieved recently is..........
27. Something I have learned to do recently is.......
28. Something I think is good about being a boy/girl is.....
29. Something I would like to do again is...........
30. Something I will never do again........
31. Something I avoid doing is........
32. When kids make mistakes teachers should........

Wishes.

1. I wish I could.........
2. If I had three wishes...
3. A hobby I wish I could do is......
4. A sport I wish I could do is.
5. A place I wish I could visit is....
6. Someone I wish I could meet is......
7. Something I wish I could do is......
8. When I was little I used to wish.......
9. Now what I wish for is................
10. When I grow up I wish to be...............
11. Something I wish for my family is...........
12. Something I wish for my class is............
13. Something I wish for this school is............
14. I wish my parents would let me...........

Feelings.

1. Today I feel....
2. I feel ....about myself.
3. I feel ....about Circle Time.
4. I feel............the future.
5. I feel.........about this school/school rules.
6. I feel........about society.
7. I feel ....about adults/teachers.
8. I feel good about......
9. I feel bad about......
10. I feel ....about my name.
11. I feel.............about my appearance.
12. I feel............about war/drugs/peace/stealing/bullying/pollution/ violence/the environment/cars.
13. I feel good/happy/pleased when........
14. I feel sad/bad/unhappy/angry/miserable when..........
15a. A time I felt afraid was.....and it was fun.
15b. A time I felt afraid was..............and it was not fun.
16. When I first came to school I felt...........
17. Before I came to this school I felt...........
18. New experiences/the unknown makes me feel..........
19. I feel powerless when............
20. I feel helpless when...........
21. I feel lonely when.........
22. .... makes me feel happy/sad/pleased.
              helpless/angry/miserable
23. I feel concerned for........
24. Making decisions makes me feel........
25. If I make a mistake I feel..........
26. What I feel about mistakes is..........
27. If someone else makes a mistake I feel..........

Favourites.

1. My favourite TV programme is........
2. My favourite book is........
3. My favourite computer programme is......
4. My favourite food is........
5. My favourite meal is......
6. My favourite time of the year is........
7. My favourite person in my family is.........
8. My favourite pop/TV star is........
9. My favourite time at home is..........
10. My favourite time at school is.........
11. My favourite time is.......
12. My favourite game to play is.......
13. My favourite things to do with my friends is......
14. My favourite possession is.....
15. My favourite toy is.......
16. My favourite place in my house is......
17. My favourite place to go is......
18. My favourite type of weather is........
19. My favourite thing to wear is........

Personal Skills.

1. I like myself least when...
2. I like myself when......
3. At home I am good at.......
4. In school I am good at.....
5. I like doing....
6. At home I am not very good at...
7. At school I am not very good at.....
8. I dislike doing......
9. Something I like doing but am not very good at is.......
10. Something I had to work hard to learn was.......
11. Something I intend learning is....
12. I am at my best ....
13. Something that was a hard decision for me was.....
14. I would like to take responsibility at home for....
15. I would like to take responsibility at school for....
16. A time I was given responsibility was...... and I did it very well.
17. A time I was given responsibility was ....and it did not work out/was too much.
18. Something I am proud of is........
19a. A limitation I can accept in myself is......
19b. A limitation I hate in myself is....
19c. A limitation I could change is.....
20. Something I did and can be proud of........
21. If I could turn the clock back to change something I did it would be.........

Conclusion.

You can obviously create your own sentence completion to suit your group but remember that like all skills they will develop with practice. You will start with sentences that are non threatening; *"My favourite TV programme is.."* As the pupils gain the skills of the language of feelings you can move onto more disclosing statements, *"Today I feel.. "* When you feel confident that the group is secure you can more onto statements, *"I feel...about my appearance".*

Silent statements can be used to allow pupils to self disclose without using words.

GAMES AND ACTIVITIES.

The games and activities complement the material found in Circle Time (1993). As your group becomes confident with using the circle you can provide activities that start outside and later discuss them within the circle.

COMMUNICATION.

Finger Talk.

Game 1: Children turn to right or left in the circle so that they are looking at the back of the person in front. A simple message is written or drawn by the facilitator onto the back of the first person. This is repeated all the way round the circle until it reaches the last person who interprets the message to the group.

Game 2: Children sit as in Game 1 but a single letter or short word is drawn on the back of the person in front and the last person guesses it.

Game 3: Children sit in the circle holding hands, lightly, to be ready to receive and send messages. A series of squeezes – like Morse code – are sent round the circle. The last person can choose whether or not to tap out the rhythm.

Co-operation.

Web of Friendship.

Material needed: A fairly large ball of wool.

The facilitator wraps wool round her wrist then passes or throws the ball of wool to someone saying *"I am passing it to ..... because....."*

You can decide what the positive reason is. For example it may be a positive attribute such as something she does well or the reason that person makes a good friend. Another reason for passing the wool could be something they know they have in common. Each participant must make sure they hold onto the wool. As the ball of wool goes back and forth across the room a web builds up. You then have a visible sign of the connections between the children and the web that binds them together. Reasons for choosing someone to pass the wool to could include:

> A skill e.g. good at football / maths
> A personal attribute e.g. thoughtful
> A kind deed e.g. looked after me.

Information sharing – pairs.

It can be very threatening for children to share information with the whole group. It is also very difficult to "boast" about our accomplishments to the whole class. However, it is much easier to tell one other person and to allow her to pass on this information. You can use all the sentence completion ideas in this way. The dialogue used in this exercise will encourage reflection and thought. It will help self-concept and self-awareness and will give participants practice in passing on positive information about someone else. You can also give children separate exercises on listening. Bliss and Tetley (1993) page 23 Game 3.

Mirroring Game.

Place children into pairs. Try, where possible, to organise pairs of children who do not normally associate together. Label them A and B. Tell As to talk about a time they remember having fun. Tell Bs to listen but to mirror A's body language whilst they are talking. Allow approximately one minute then let the children swap roles.

Return to the circle to ask them to say,

> * what it felt like to copy the speaker.
> * what it felt like to be copied while they where speaking.
> * did they become aware of their own body language while doing this exercise?
> * did anything surprise them about this exercise?

You may like to model this with a pupil so that the group is clear about the activity.

Mixing up Games.

These are very useful for separating friends and moving groups of pupils who might, if they sit together, be silly. You can use a mixing up game at any time if you think that you have an inappropriate group of pupils sitting together.

Change places if you have;
* a brother
* a sister
* a dog etc.
* are wearing brown shoes
* are wearing black shoes.

You can use more directive activities, give each pupils the name of a set of;
* cars - Rover, Jaguar, Honda
* transport - train, boat, plane
* salad bowl - tomato, cucumber, lettuce etc.

When you say a specific name, e.g. Jaguar, all children who have been identified as Jaguars change places, when you say 'cars' everybody changes places.

Another mixing up game is Postman. Give each child a number from 1 to the number of pupils in the circle.

You can ask,
* all even numbers to change places
* all odd numbers to change places.

You can give specific numbers, e.g. numbers 1, 9, 16, 19, and 32 change places. To get everyone to change places say the postman calls or delivery.

Developing Themes.

As your group grows in confidence you can develop various themes; co-operation, self-concept, friendship, bullying, equal opportunities...

Developing Themes 1 - Co-operative Activities.

Co-operation means working together.

This is a theme we use with all groups of children fairly early in their development. Co-operation is something that is demanded by the N.C. and needs to be taught. It requires a certain level of maturity and the possession of certain social skills for it to work in a truly co-operative and collaborative way.

The games will encourage the group to;

* understand what co-operation means
* practise and analyse what happens in co-operation
* learn how it feels to work co-operatively.

Teachers should check with their groups that they are making the connection between the activity and what it is they are supposed to be learning. The counterchecking of what happens when we do not co-operate will help with this. Circle games are a fun way to learn but it is important to relate the activity to the consequences and then generalise them into everyday life. This particular theme often requires rather more explaining and direction from the teachers than most other themes.

Partners.

Instruct the group to ask the person sitting on their left how they are feeling today. Then partners will introduce one another saying how that person feels e.g. *"This is Robert, he is feeling very happy today."*

Sentence Completion.

Explain that you intend taking a theme today and what it is. Co-operation is about working together, helping other people, being concerned for another person and trying to help them.
You could start with sentence completion:

I helped ... by .....
I worked with ... and we did .....
I co-operated with ... when we did .....

You can also explore areas where the pupils did not co-operate.

I didn't co-operate when I ......

As you develop the theme of co-operation you can move onto,

Co-operation is important because ......
We need to know how to co-operate because .....

Thunder. (the video, "Coming round to Circle Time" shows this activity)

In the early stages of co-operation you can get the group to follow instructions contributing to a whole circle activity. Start by modelling actions that are copied by all group members.

"I was walking in a forest. It was a warm, sunny day but suddenly the weather changed. The wind started blowing (rub your hands together, the group follows your example). As the wind got stronger the rain started to fall gently (now pat two fingers into your palm). The rain started to pour out of the sky (now clap your hands). The thunder started, it made the whole earth shake (start stamping your feet). Then the thunder stopped (revert to clapping your hands), the rain became gentler (stop clapping your hands and tap two fingers in your palm). The weather kept improving, until there was just a gentle breeze blowing (rub your hands together) and then the sun started shining again, (stop rubbing hands together)."

This ends the activity.

Other Co-operative Activities.

You can start many co-operative activities outside the circle, and then form the circle to find out how the activity made the participants feel.

* People Balance.
* Ways we co-operate.
* Co-operative Tessellations. (see section Games and Activities that start outside the circle.)

Developing Themes 2 - Self Concept Activities.

We have identified various sentence completion statements that begin to develop the pupils' feelings of self. They all focus on two major aspects,

* I am .....
* I feel .....

Other activities such as:

* My Achievements
* My Goals
* Who I am

all help to focus on the individual.

The following activities are also useful for developing Self Concept.

Partners.

Within the circle divide pupils into pairs. If there is an odd number pair yourself with a pupil.

Partners 1. Get the pairs to identify what they are good at and then report back to the group one thing their partner is good at.

Partners 2.

Ask each person to identify to their partner three things that they can do.

This can be specific;

* Three things you can do at school.
* Three things you can do at home etc.

Get the partner to identify to the group what the other can do.

Partners 3.

Discover something that your partner has learned to do recently and report back to the group.

Special Person.

Identify one person to go out of the room. Place a large sheet on the floor and go round the group asking each person to make a positive statement about the special person. Write down the comments and then ask the special person to return.

If appropriate, you might ask them to sit in the middle of the circle and the group can then make their positive statement. If you think the pupil would find it difficult to sit in this isolated position, allow her to take her place in the circle. The sheet of paper can be displayed in the classroom, perhaps under a heading "This Week's Special Person". At the end of the week the sheet can be taken home.

Photographs.

Photographs 1.

We find photographs a very positive way to celebrate individuals. If you take a photograph of each child at the start of the year, their photograph could be attached to "This Week's Special Person".

Photographs 2.

Ask the children to bring a photograph of themselves alone or included in a family group. In the circle each child holds up her photograph and describes the picture.

"This is me when I was ....."

"I chose this photograph because ....."

Children love to be identified as individuals. You can use the photographs to make displays.

Photographs 3.

Ask the pupils to bring in photographs of themselves as babies. Display these on large sheets of paper and ask the class to guess and write down who they think the baby is.

Photographs 4.

Ask the pupils to bring a photograph of themselves and display on large sheets of paper. Get the other pupils to write positive comments underneath the photograph.

GAMES AND ACTIVITIES THAT START OUTSIDE THE CIRCLE.

As you become more confident using Circle Time you can develop various ideas. You can get the pupils to set goals for themselves, to engage in co-operative games and to identify their achievements. These activities might start with the pupils at their desks completing worksheets, or in the cleared classroom doing co-operative or trust games. When the activity is completed the pupils could, in a circle, talk about their reactions to the activity.

My Achievements.

Explain about achievements that are appropriate for the age group. Give out worksheet one and ask the children to fill in one or two achievements inside the body shape. Split into pairs and talk about achievements. Ask the partner to think about the other person and make a further suggestion as to what their partner has achieved. If they cannot think of a suggestion because they do not know the partner very well, suggest trigger questions

"Tell me something that you are pleased with that you've done recently."

"Has the teacher been pleased with you recently?"

"Has you parent/carer been pleased with you?"

"Have you been nice to your brother/sister?"

Encourage the class to ask positive questions to find out what their partner has achieved. You could be specific by asking all the pupils to identify achievements;

* in school

* at home

* in leisure pursuits.

Activity 1.

Each child feeds back, to the whole group, her partner's achievements.

Activity 2.

Each child feeds back, to the whole group, her own achievements.

Activity 3.

Art Gallery - Display all the sheets and allow the pupils to circulate and read the achievements of their classmates. Reconvene the group and do a sentence completion.

"One thing I found surprising was ....."

"I learned that ..... has achieved ....."

My Goals.

You could begin to get the pupils to start thinking about setting goals by sentence completion.

"Today I plan to do ......"
"Tomorrow I intend to do ....."
"It's good/useful to have goals because ....."

Discussion should include ideas about having goals set at the right level for us as individuals and encouraging children to think in realistic terms. Also the fact that we do not usually set the same standard of goals for every area of our lives e.g. we would not all hope to become star football players whereas reasonable competence in ball skills such as throwing and catching might be a good goal. We cannot all be Einstein at maths but we could set small goals such as understanding division to 20 by the end of term. Small attainable goals will give us a feeling of success when we achieve them, as will specific targets. Huge unattainable goals will reinforce failure quite unnecessarily. This can also be discussed.

* Use worksheet two simply as personal goals/aims for the children.
* Put groups into pairs to discuss their goals/aims. They then report back to the group the goals of the partner.

Note: You may need to model this to the pupils. You could provide some of the goals/aims that are appropriate for the age, and then set personal goals/aims. You can decide whether the goal is a very short term one, something to aim for today or this week. With older pupils you might ask them to identify a short term goal and long term goal.

People Balance.

These are co-operative games that are fun.

Game 1.
Children sit in pairs, back to back with arms linked. They then stand up in this position. They will need to support each other in order to do this.

Game 2.
Children sit in a group of four, back to back, arms linked. The group tries to stand up. They will need to be aware of one another's movements and weight.

Game 3.
Children sit facing one another, legs straight, feet touching, holding hands. They try to help each other to stand. They must not let go of each others' hands. This can be done as a foursome but it is not always successful in the way Game 2 is. The pupils can then come back into the circle and describe how they felt doing these co-operative activities.

Ways we Co-operate.

Activity 1.
Talk about co-operating, how you co-operate and how they co-operate. Split into threes and give out worksheet three. Ask them to discuss how they co-operate with friends, family members, teacher. They can write in as many things as they can think of.
Allow time to discuss and give them notice of three minutes to finish the activity.
Reconvene the large circle and ask each member of the triad to say one thing from each of the circles on the worksheet.

Activity 2.
Talk about ways people don't co-operate, how easy it is to be awkward. Give examples. Give out sheet 4. Repeat as Activity 1.

Being Called Names.

Split the group into threes and get them to complete worksheet 5. Ask them to consider name calling and to list as many reasons as they can think of why people want to call others unpleasant names. Allow the group to decide who will write down the responses.

Reconvene the circle and ask each person to state one reason why other people name-call. You can then move on to a sentence completion.

"When I was called a name I felt ......"
"I think people who call names are ......"

Other Activities.

After the groups of three's have completed their worksheets, combine the groups of three into groups of six and ask them to compare their responses. Then reconvene the circle and discuss the findings from the worksheets.

Bullying.

This might already have been covered in the circle with Silent Statements.

      * Change places all those who have seen bullying in this school.

      * Change places all those who have seen bullying in this class.

and/or Sentence Completion:

      * Knowing about bullying makes me feel .....

      * I think a person who is bullied feels .....

      * I think a person who bullies is ......

      * When bullying happens I feel .....

You could develop this work with worksheet 6. The pupils could complete the worksheets individually, then come into groups of four to discuss their responses. Reconvene the group and get individuals to make one comment about where bullying happens. Go round the group and then ask for responses about when bullying happens followed by what happens. You can develop this group awareness about bullying by moving from - *"we accept bullying happens"* to - *"what we can do about it"*.

Sentence Completion.

    The next time I see bullying happen I will do .....

Group work

Split into groups of three. Give out a worksheet 6b. If bullying happens we could do .....

Ask the group to make as many suggestions as possible.

After five minutes combine the groups of three in to groups of six. Get the larger group to compare their responses. After ten minutes reconvene the circle to discuss the responses.

Follow up Work.

    (1) You might want to produce a bullying policy for your class.

    (2) You might want to get the pupils to discuss what they want from the classroom.

I have a right in this class

    * *to be listened to*

    * *to feel safe*

    * *not to be put down.*

Split the class into fours and get them to discuss together what they need to feel safe and to learn effectively. Reconvene the class and get them to state what they feel their rights are to learn effectively. Produce your own unique class statement;

    I have a right in this class .....

Who I Am.

The pupils need either a photograph of themselves, or, if this is not possible, a small drawing of themselves. (You could for a small cost take a photograph of each pupil or even get the pupils to take the photographs.)

You could prepare the worksheets by sticking on the children's photographs or drawings. If the pupils are capable, they could do the sticking themselves.

You could use yourself as an example and show the pupils who you are. Draw arrows from the picture to identify aspects of yourself, the house you live in, what you like, what you hate (see worksheets seven or eight).

We have provided an example. You could be prescriptive and give the headings you want the children to complete or allow them to develop their own ideas. Reconvene the group and discuss the worksheets.

The pupils could:

Activity 1 - Hold up their sheets and identify two or three significant aspects of themselves.

Activity 2 - Discuss their sheets with their partner who then tells the group one thing new she learned about her partner.

Art Gallery - All the sheets are displayed around the room. The pupils go round, look at the sheets and try and find something they didn't know about other members of the class.

The circle reconvenes and each pupil completes a sentence.

"One thing I learned about ...... was ...."

Co-operative Tessellations.

The following activities create situations in which the children need to co-operate to complete the task successfully. Worksheets 9 -18: photo-copy, or create your own tessellations onto thin card. (Keep a copy of the completed tessellation so that you remember what the finished product looks like!)

Rules for the Games:

1) No speaking is allowed.

2) No touching, tapping or other kind of body contact.

3) No begging looks or gestures.

4) You may be given a piece but you are not allowed to snatch.

5) No one is in charge.

Activity 1.

Explain the rules of the game. Divide the class into groups of four or five. Give each group a tessellation cut into pieces. They have to put the pieces into a complete set. (If the pupils are very young or inexperienced you could give them a photocopy of the completed set.)

Activity 2.

Give each pupil one piece of a puzzle. (The number of puzzles you use will depend on the size of your class.) Place photocopies of the completed puzzle around the room and the pupils have to find where their piece fits. Then they have to find other pupils whose pieces will help complete the whole puzzle. (Remind them of the rules.)

Activity 3.

You can make the activity as complicated as you like, depending on the experience/ability of your pupils. You could tell them we have three puzzles to complete, and provide no help other than the framework of the puzzle. (Remind them of the rules.) You might use pages 10, 12, and 15 which are quite different, but you could use pages 12, 13 and 14 which are similar, or you can set a time limit, such as five minutes.

Reconvene the circle. You then could use Sentence Completion exercises:

"I found this activity to be......."

"The hardest part of this activity was......."

or general discussion about co-operation:

* How difficult/easy it is to co-operate

* Thinking about other tasks that need co-operation.

YOUR QUESTIONS ANSWERED.

HOW TO USE CIRCLE TIME.

Where should it take place?

In your classroom. It keeps the happy and warm atmosphere you generate at Circle Time in your class.

How much room do you need?

Room to make a proper circle, to enable pupils and teachers to make eye contact and facilitate full participation in every interaction.

How should I organise the circle?

We believe that all participants should sit on chairs. The chairs help create the boundary. If the pupils sit on the floor the boundary becomes fluid which makes organisation difficult.

How disruptive is Circle Time to my normal class routine?

It does take some organisation, but your pupils will become more skilled with practice. Some teachers find it easier to organise first thing in the morning, or after a break. One teacher we know continues her circle working with music, another follows her Circle Time with a story.

What equipment do I need?

Other than you, the space and the confidence to try it, nothing. As you develop Circle Time you may need to prepare some worksheets to stimulate thought and discussion.

How long should it take?

The maximum time is about 30 minutes. If your class is new to Circle Time you may start with 15 minute sessions.

How should I organise Circle Time?

We find it useful in the beginning to start and end with fun activities. As with any skill you start with easy activities and lead gradually into more demanding tasks. Even when your class is used to Circle Time we feel it is important to have a definite closing activity, and we usually try to make this less demanding in terms of self-disclosure.

What happens if the children copy what others have said?

Don't worry; this is part of normal development. Children are learning how to express themselves, and to learn we often model ourselves on others. In time the young people will feel confident to express their own views and will have learnt the language of self-expression.

Some children might always "pass". How do I respond to this?

Each pupil has a right to pass. Accept this and don't worry. Some people find it easier than others to make statements. If you watch carefully you will usually find the pupils who are passing are listening to the others. At the end of a round always go back to the pupils who have passed and ask if they now wish to contribute. Don't put any pressure on the pupils if they choose to remain silent.

How can I develop Circle Time?

This is a process which grows with the group and the confidence to maintain development depends upon the security achieved in the early stages. It starts with the pupils becoming confident about being in a circle and learning to speak for themselves and listen to others. When the group feels confident and secure you can move onto more challenging activities. You can start activities and tasks outside the circle and then use the circle to discuss and reflect upon what the individuals / group have done and learned.

How can Circle Time be introduced to the whole school?

It is important to realise that Circle Time is a process, and that the level of skills the pupils display is not only dependent on their maturity. We have provided plans that will guide you through schemes of work and record keeping. If you feel that cognitive performance is worth planning and recording, then social development should be given the same value. You should be looking for stages that initially concentrate on speaking and listening (this could be in year 1 or year 6, depending on how much experience the pupils have of Circle Time.) However, we would expect if the pupils have experience of being exposed to circle experiences by year 6/7, they will be given the trust to begin to organise for themselves what happens in the circle.

How do I introduce the rules?

The rules of Circle Time should "evolve". You need to introduce certain rules immediately, the most important one being,

    * we listen when someone else is speaking.

You can introduce other rules such as "no put downs" as the need arises.

WHY USE CIRCLE TIME?

In their article on pastoral work in schools Askew and Carnell (1995) describe a difference between;

> "..the 'school centred' which emphasises social control and regulation, and 'pupil centred', which emphasises negotiation and social awareness."
> (page 28)

We hope we have justified that we feel activities such as Circle Time have a crucial role to play in the development of young people. Education is more than the transmission of information. This is important but so is a supportive, emotional approach. We need to encourage young people to want to be in schools and to enjoy their learning. Writers such as Rutter (1991) highlight that schools can help counter stress and difficulties in all aspects of children's lives;

> "it is not high school achievement as such that seems to make a difference, rather, it is positive experiences of a kind that are pleasurable and rewarding and which help children develop a sense of their own worth together with the confidence that they can cope with life's challenges and can control what happens to them." (p.8)

We believe that positive experiences such as Circle Time have a long term effect. It's not easy to justify this statement, but Rutter (1991) writes....

> "It's no easy matter to create a happy, effective school and there are a variety of influences outside the control of schools. Nevertheless, schooling does matter greatly. Moreover, the benefits can be surprisingly long-lasting. That is not because school experiences have a permanent effect on a child's psychological brain structure, but rather because experiences at one point in a child's life tend to influence what happens afterwards in a complicated set of indirect chain reactions."

What are the benefits of Circle Time?

We believe that:

* You will learn a lot more about your pupils.
* Your pupils will learn a lot more about themselves and how they operate in groups.
* They will learn how to express themselves.
* Relationships in the classroom will improve, between you and the pupils, and between the pupils.
* It is an enjoyable time that the pupils look forward to.

The effects both short term and long term are indicated by Rutter (1991). Most schools in their policy documents or mission statements identify aspects of personal development as well as the transmission of knowledge. Circle Time establishes a means of assisting personal and non-academic learning.

"positive school experiences of both academic and non-academic kinds can have protective effect for children under stress and living otherwise unrewarding lives. These last points remind us once again that school provides a set of a social experience for children as well as a place for scholastic learning, and that effective schools have both aspects of children's lives as part of their goals" (p 9)

Circle Time can be a rewarding experience for all participants, including you.

BIBLIOGRAPHY.

Askew, S. and Carnell, E., (1995) Approaches to work with Individual Young People.
Pastoral Care in Education. March 1995.

Ballard, J.,(1982) Circlebook.
Irvington, New York.

Bliss, T. & Tetley, J., (1993) Circle Time.
Lucky Duck Publishing.

Bliss, T., Robinson, G. and Maines, B., (1995) Coming Round to Circle Time, (Video).
Lucky Duck Publications.

Canfield, J. and Wells, H., (1976) 100 Ways to Enhance Self Concept in the Classroom.
Prentice-Hall, Englewood Cliffs, New Jersey.

Curry, M. & Bromfield, C., (1994) Personal and Social Education for Primary Schools through Circle Time.
NASEN Enterprises Ltd.

Fountain, S., (1990) Learning Together: Global Education.
Stanley Thomas.

Gordon, T., (1974) Teacher Effectiveness Training.
David McKay.

Johnson, D. & Johnson F., (1987) Joining Together.
Prentice Hall.

Lawrence, D., (1988) Enhancing Self-esteem in the Classroom.
Paul Chapman Publishing Ltd.

Mosley, J., (1993) Turn your school around.
L.D.A.

National Curriculum Council, (1993) Spiritual and Moral Development - a discussion paper.

Rutter, M., (1991) Pathways from Childhood to Adult Life.
Pastoral Care in Education. Vol. 9 No. 3

Tuckman, B., (1965) Developmental sequence in small groups.
Psychological Bulletin, 63, 384-399.

White, M., (1992) Self-esteem, its meaning and value in schools.
Daniels Publishing.

APPENDIX.

1   My Achievements.
2   My Goals.
3   Ways we co-operate.
4   Ways we do not co-operate.
5   Name Calling.
6. Bullying.
       a Where, when and what happens.
       b If bullying happens we could.
7   Who I am, an example.
8   Who I am, proforma.
9-18   Tessellations.

For more information and a fast growing slection of
Circle Time resources contact us at:

Lucky Duck Publishing Ltd.

34 Wellington Park
Bristol BS8 2UW

Phone or Fax 0117 9732881 or 01454 776620
e-mail publishing@luckyduck.co.uk
website www.luckyduck.co.uk

WORKSHEET 1

My achievements ...

WORKSHEET 2

My goals are ...

Ways I co-operate with ...

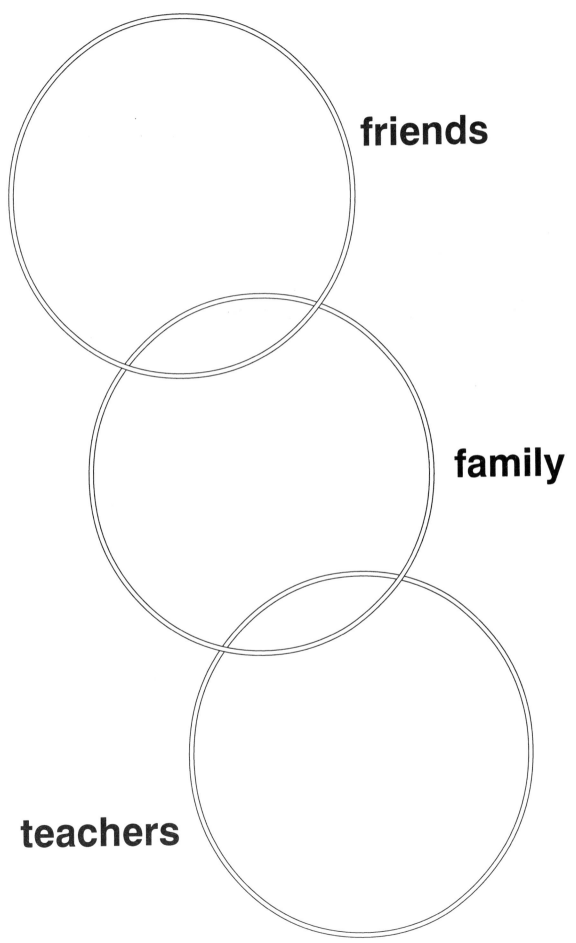

friends

family

teachers

Ways I do not co-operate with ...

friends

family

teachers

WORKSHEET 5

Name Calling - why it happens...

BULLYING -

> where it happens...

> when it happens...

> what happens...

BULLYING -

if bullying happens we could:

WORKSHEET 7

Who I am....

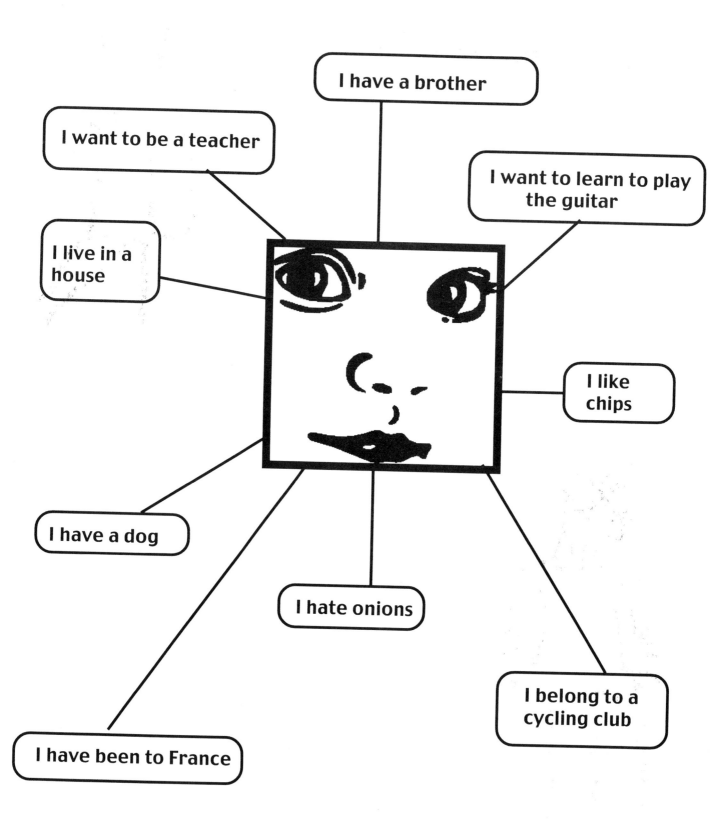

I have a brother

I want to be a teacher

I want to learn to play the guitar

I live in a house

I like chips

I have a dog

I hate onions

I belong to a cycling club

I have been to France

Who I am....

Your own photo
or a self-portrait

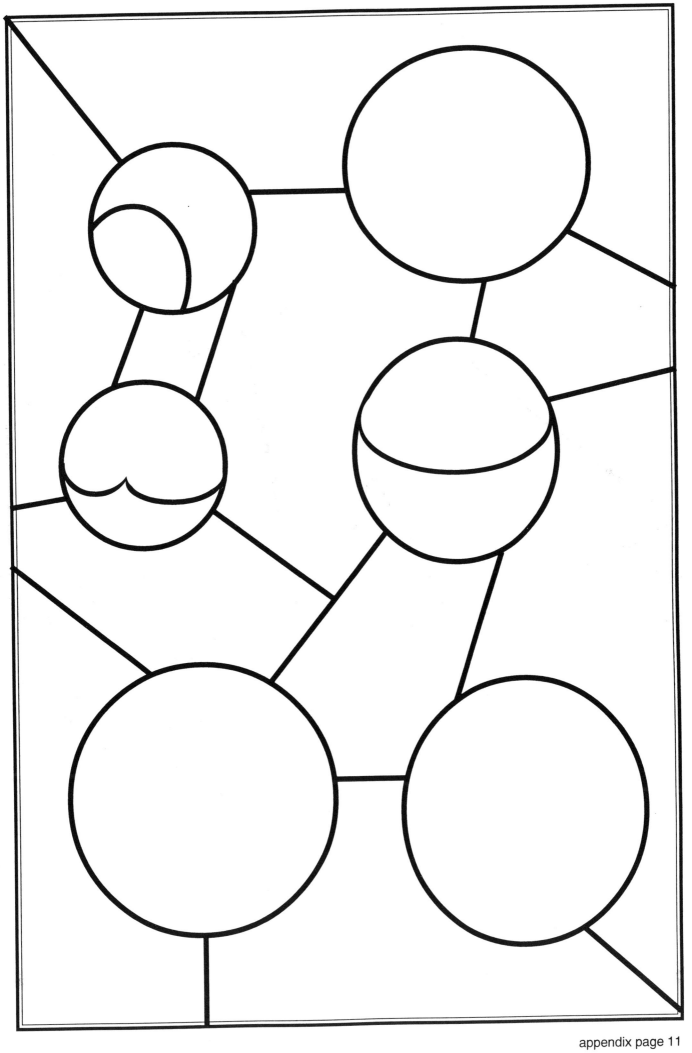

appendix page 14

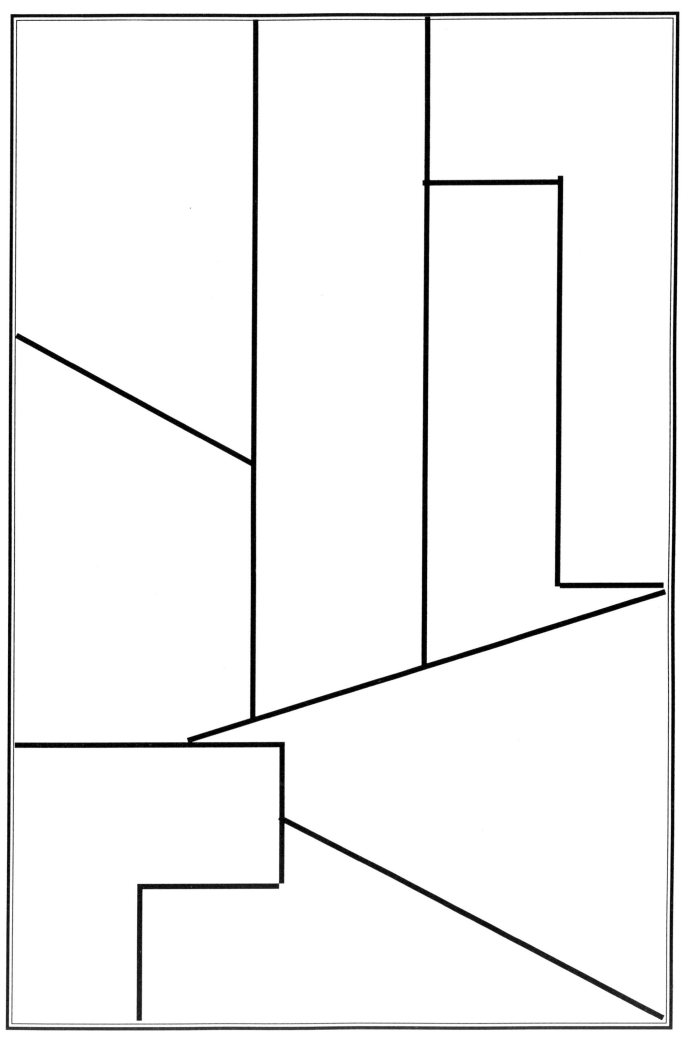

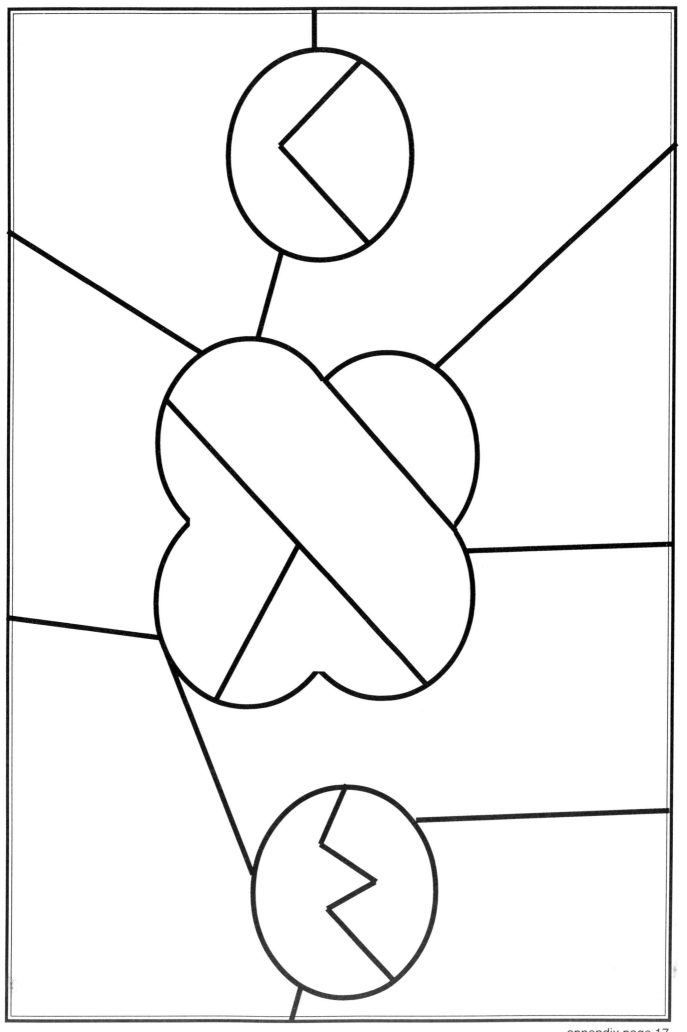

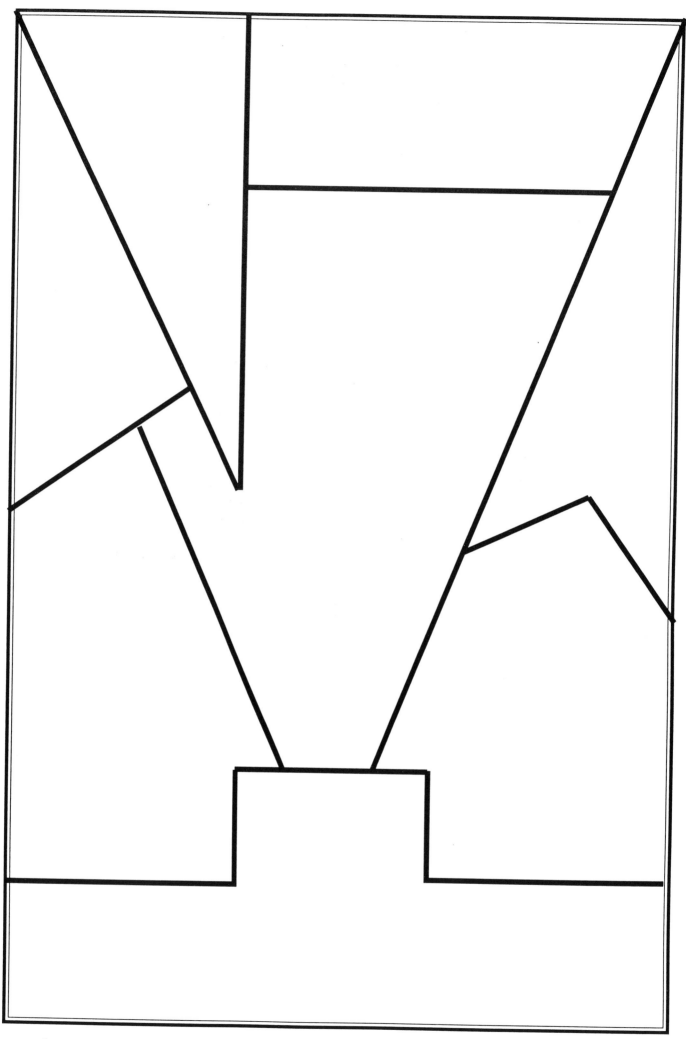

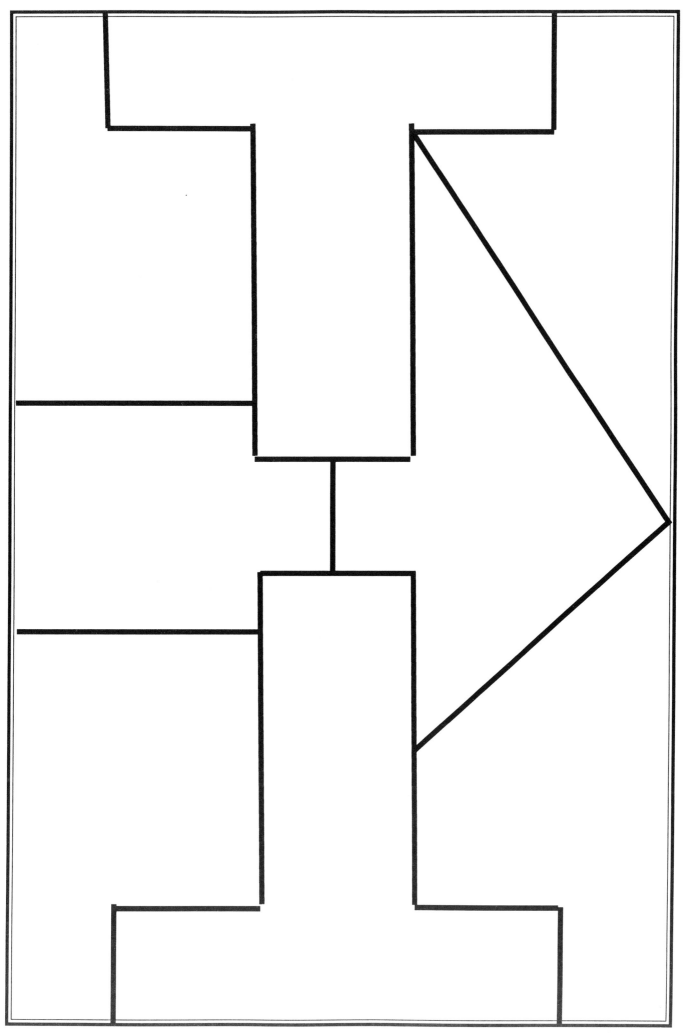